240
15⁰⁰

| JOSEF KLEIN |
| S C U L P T U R E S |

D1026702

GEORGIA
MUSEUM
OF · ART

THE UNIVERSITY OF GEORGIA

Cover: Josef Klein (American, b. Germany, 1902-1992)
           Slave, 1930-34
           Terra cotta
           12½ inches
           Estate of the Artist

©1995 Georgia Museum of Art, University of Georgia.
Published by the Georgia Museum of Art, University of Georgia.
All rights reserved. No part of the contents of this book may be
reproduced without the written consent of the publishers.

Josef Klein Sculptures
Design: Kudzu Graphics
Body Copy: Utopia (Adobe), Heads/Folio: Geometric 231 (Bitstream)
Director of Publications: Bonnie Ramsey
Printed in an edition of 1,000 by University Printing,
University of Georgia

Library of Congress No. Applied for at the Cataloging in Publication
Division of the Library of Congress
ISBN 0-915977-19-2

This project is supported in part by a Senior Research Grant from
the University of Georgia Research Foundation. Partial support for
the exhibitions and programs at the Georgia Museum of Art is provided by the Georgia Council for the Arts through appropriations of the
Georgia General Assembly and the National Endowment for the Arts.
A portion of the museum's general operating funds for this fiscal year
has been provided through a grant from the Institute of Museum
Services, a federal agency that offers general operating support to
the nation's museums.

GEORGIA
MUSEUM
OF·ART

TABLE OF CONTENTS

FOREWORD

What becomes most apparent from the essay in this catalogue, and from the exhibition which it accompanies is the abiding belief of Josef Klein in art's power not only to engage the viewer but to inspire him or her as well. Professor William T. Squires has been similarly devoted to Klein's art; he has pursued the sometimes elusive truths of Klein's life and career on two continents, with our audiences as the happy beneficiaries of this quest. Professor Squires has collaborated with the staff of the Georgia Museum of Art to assign Josef Klein his appropriate place in the history of 20th-century American art, and, in so doing, has rescued an important figure in Georgia's cultural life from the neglect of unintentional forgetfulness. We applaud and acknowledge his efforts and are grateful to the sculptor's family for the assistance they gave Professor Squires.

WILLIAM U. EILAND
DIRECTOR

ACKNOWLEDGEMENTS

This exhibition is made possible by the enthusiastic support of Gloria Frame and Siegfried Klein, the daughter and son of the sculptor. Both Professor Renato Carozzi of the Accademia Reale di Belle Arti and artist/critic Luciano Lattanzi of Carrara, Italy, were instrumental in completing the pivotal "Carrara connection" of this study. Slavica Velikonja of the Amidas Agency in Ljubljana, Slovenia, assisted with translation and interpretation of documents from Carrara. Aurelia Ghezzi and Barbara Cooper of the University of Georgia translated Italian and German documents from the Klein estate. Lynnette Aldrich of the School of Art provided talent and good-natured patience in preparing the manuscript for publication.

Without the support of a Senior Research Grant from the University of Georgia Research Foundation, the scope of this project would be limited and incomplete. Dr. Evan Firestone and colleagues of the School of Art granted me sufficient space and time in which to bring this project to fruition, and Dr. Donald Keyes of the Georgia Museum of Art worked diligently with me to help produce an exhibition and catalogue of enduring quality and beauty.

WILLIAM T. SQUIRES

INTRODUCTION

Josef Klein thought of himself as a great sculptor, a modern heir apparent to Michelangelo, claiming his line of descent through the renowned marble quarries in Carrara, Italy, where he studied with Carlo Fontana. Klein's patrons, friends, and art critics conspired by passing the "mantle of greatness" to him through more than a dozen contemporary newspaper and magazine accounts in which he is called "famous," "a great man," "a modern genius." One frequently finds references to him as "eminent," "celebrated," "outstanding," "noted," and "distinguished." But today, fifty years later, he is all but forgotten.

Who was Josef Klein? Of what significance is his work? What is the relationship between his aspirations as a sculptor, his quest for celebrity, and the quality of his work? This exhibition addresses the questions of significance and quality by revealing much about taste and public commissions in Atlanta in the 1930s. It exposes the hardships faced by an immigrant German sculptor working in America during the Depression and the role of arrogance in the failed career of a fascinating character. Finally, the exhibition allows a careful scrutiny of Klein's sculpture, without the earlier hyperbole attached to his career.

Klein created the bulk of the works in the exhibition in Atlanta. They date from 1928 through 1939, with the latest drawings in the exhibition dating from 1942. Klein completed the earliest sculptures in the exhibition between 1928 and 1930, when he lived in Jacksonville, Florida.

Klein was always a figurative sculptor, although in the 1930s he made several ventures into Art Deco abstractions incorporating elements of Cubism and Futurism. Klein's real talent was as a modeler in clay and a carver of reliefs. His facility at modeling portraits was so great that he frequently held public sessions during which he would select a member of the audience as his subject and fashion a portrait bust in clay as the crowd watched. One afternoon in Miami, Florida, a gawking crowd saw Klein model a portrait of former heavyweight boxing champion Jack Dempsey. The boxer enjoyed the event and liked Klein's work so well that he purchased the completed terra cotta bust.

Klein's proposals and actual commissions were either monuments and/or portraits. Additionally, he sculpted traditional subjects such as youths, mothers and children, dancers, and wrestlers. There are religious figures Klein created such as *Hand from the Cross,* (plate 29), several crucifixions, and busts of Christ. Only one of Klein's monumental projects exists today: his huge bronze statue of U. S. Senator Thomas E. Watson, on the Georgia State Capitol grounds in Atlanta. He completed at least one other large-scale project in plaster, which he abandoned when he left Atlanta in 1950. He made several proposals for additional large scale sculptures in the 1930s, but these were either rejected or accepted but not funded. Portraiture was Klein's bread and butter. He modeled and carved busts and bas reliefs of famous people, local dignitaries, his children, and himself. Shortly after arriving in Atlanta in 1930, Klein pursued several grandiose projects; however, ten years later, embittered and not yet forty, he refused to seek any sculptural commissions. Proposals for commissions Klein made as late as 1939 were not accepted. Promised commissions did not materialize. As the economic depression deepened in the late 1930s, there were few sculptural commissions awarded in Atlanta.

By the age of forty, and living in grinding poverty, Klein's career as a sculptor was effectively over. He became increasingly private, hoarding and refusing to sell work he had completed years earlier. When he died in 1992 at the age of ninety, his estate included more than two hundred sketches, drawings, designs, paintings, and one hundred sculptural works dating from 1928 until 1942. Were Klein still alive, this retrospective exhibition could not take place; he would not have allowed it.

Josef Klein was a curious mix of arrogance, insecurity, and naiveté. Upon his arrival in the Southeast, he was determined to elevate what he saw as a culturally blighted American South through his protean talent. Although his expectations were inflated, they were based in some measure on substantial training and experience in Germany, France, and Italy. Fortunately, Klein's activities during the 1930s in Atlanta are well documented in newspapers and photographs, and in addition, he kept autobiographical notes beginning with a manuscript written in Paris in 1927 and added to as late as 1942 in Atlanta. In his youth Klein was a blatant self-promoter who later became a reclusive, eccentric old man.

Hints of his melancholic withdrawal are evident in a brief sketch he wrote in Atlanta: "My works are my idols; they speak to me; they are my brain-children, my mistakes, subject to evolution with an ever-changing mood, ever changing light." Similar anecdotal accounts provide valuable insights about not only Klein's expectations as a youth, but also the later disillusionment that precipitated an early end to his career as a sculptor.

Although Klein's career as a sculptor must be judged on the basis of work completed in the brief span of a dozen years, sufficient evidence remains to assess his contribution. This exhibition focuses on the most productive years of Klein's career, the early and mid-1930s in Atlanta.

The sculptures and drawings in the exhibition represent less than one-quarter of Klein's total *oeuvre* of over 150 works. Inventories of his work and sales records were either not kept by Klein or have been lost or destroyed. Because their whereabouts are unknown, none of Klein's European works are in the exhibition, including an important German sculptural commission, the carved marble bust of Hans Brauns, Imperial Prime Minister of Germany, made during the late 1920s. In addition, Klein was reportedly one of four sculptors who collaborated on a monumental statue of Mussolini erected in the Palazzo of the Dictator in Rome. While no drawings or photographs have been found which confirm this collaboration, Klein spoke of it during interviews.

The catalogue and many of the works from the *Art-Salon of 1934*, sponsored by the Business and Professional Women's Club of Atlanta, show Klein at his artistic maturity. That exhibition, consisting of more than one hundred works, was the most comprehensive and important of Klein's career. More than one-third of those works are part of the present exhibition.

EARLY LIFE, EDUCATION & TRAVEL

Josef Klein was born on June 15, 1902, in the village of Burghagel in the district of Schwaben and Neuberg near Scheidegg, Germany.[1] He was the eldest child and only son of Josef and Genoveva Klein; he had three younger sisters, Maria, Genoveva and Berta.

Klein's family operated a small farm; in his later autobiographical notes he claims his earliest memories were of the farm, the Bavarian countryside, and his poor family. Very early in life Klein worked as a cowherd and farm hand, and later commented, "My father always found something to do; for him, one could never be busy enough."[2]

Klein loved the out-of-doors and thrived on hard, physical work. He also liked school and excelled academically, but it was manual-arts classes he particularly enjoyed.

> I had a great desire to learn, to see, to hear, and tools in my hands at a workbench made me forget the worst toothache. I showed a great deal of talent for crafts, and for that reason I became useful as an assistant, whenever structural or other repairs had to be undertaken.[3]

The seeds of Klein's artistic talent and interests were sown early by his parents. His family spent no money for toys, and one of his earliest memories is of a toy crafted by his father.

> … it was a hammer, made of wood. This hammer was supposedly my favorite toy for months. I had a great predilection for sitting on the wide window ledges of the parlor, and I would hammer with all my might and would call out with great mirth to the people who were passing by on the street below. [4]

When he was older, Klein designed and fashioned his own toys. He described in particular the making of whistles and squirt guns.

> I cut branches from the trees, peeled off the bark and cut whistles in all sizes and keys. Filbert bushes were particularly suited for that purpose. Then, I also made squirt guns from the branches of the Elderberry bush. I would cut pieces a foot long and took out the pith, I made the plunger and a small nozzle, and, there you go, the squirt gun was ready to squirt. [5]

Klein related that on both sides of his family there were amateur artists and artisans. His father's brother, Franz, a cobbler, enjoyed drawing and sketching. His grandfather was an amateur painter, and there were woodcarvers in his mother's family. Both of Klein's parents wanted him to learn a trade and to become a craftsman. This desire was consistent with the boy's early indications of talent for and interest in constructive projects such as making toys.

In his autobiographical notes, Klein humorously told how one of his youthful constructions became a part of local village lore.

> I made little waterwheels for myself and all kinds of little wooden gadgets, which then were attached to the waterwheel. I remember in particular a little hammer mill. There were about four little hammers, which hit empty tin cans, all set in motion by my waterwheel. What fun I had with that stuff. Once, if not more often, I let the hammer mill run throughout the night. As chance would have it, one night a woman came by who was very superstitious…she was walking in the vicinity of my waterwheel and suddenly she heard the thumping noise. First she stopped, then she sped up her steps, listened again, what could that be she asked herself, there surely must be some ghosts in the wood down there. She began to run, so that she was out of breath when she got home. The next morning she told her adventure and soon the whole village knew about it. First I was puzzled…But finally I saw the light, and I saw that my hammer mill was the haunted object. Naturally, I had nothing better to do than to tell about my hammer mill and a lot of laughter ensued. For a long time this ghost story circulated in the village…[6]

At age seventeen, Klein left home and traveled on foot over much of Europe for the next nine years. Occasionally, his adventures involved "misunderstandings" with local authorities. One such incident occurred in an Italian Riviera town near the French border sometime in the mid to late 1920s. Klein ran afoul of the *Fascisti* one night for his outspoken public "psychoanalysis" of Italian politics.[7] While speaking to a group of art students in a café, Klein was taken into custody by two gun-wielding fascists who only released him after the intervention of a British friend and on the condition that he immediately leave Italy. Armed guards, according to Klein, accompanied him to the border. This episode was not his first nor would it be his last run-in with authority.

During this period of Klein's youthful travels he studied architecture in Ansbach and painting and sculpture in Paris. At the end of his travels in 1928 he enrolled in classes at the Accademia Reale di Belle Arti in Carrara [fig. 1]. In an autobiographical sketch Klein wrote after 1940, he describes several high points of his travels. "... a few months after completing my architectural training, I journeyed to Italy on foot. It was in Milan that I found myself and discovered the missing link in my ambition. I fell in love with sculpture."[8]

By the age of twenty Klein had completed preparatory and master training classes at the building trades institute in Ansbach of Hans Grauf, a master architect. Documents show that Klein received top marks in his architectural studies.[9] His training established his credentials in surveying, foundations, above-ground construction, and interior and vault construction. In addition, Klein received top grades in a preparatory course for construction with stone. This course provided a grounding in the use of stone-working tools and subtractive carving techniques. Other master training courses that he completed included "Iron Construction and Public Buildings," "Structural Engineering," "Agricultural Architecture," and a course in "Project Planning."[10]

Klein intended to work professionally as an architect, and in 1923 and 1924 he designed several houses near his home town of Scheidegg. His designs were executed by his uncle, a general contractor, working with sometimes as many as 200 laborers. Between 1925 and 1927, Klein worked at a series of projects in Milan and Genoa,[11] as well as Nice, Marseilles, and Paris.[12]

Klein credited his transformation from architect to sculptor to studies at the Accademia Reale di Belle Arti in Carrara, under the neo-classically trained Italian sculptor, Carlo Fontana. When Klein arrived in Carrara, Carlo was the latest in a line of Fontanas who had taught sculpture at the Accademia from the time of its founding in 1769. Records from the Accademia show that in 1928 Klein attended Fontana's courses "Plastic Figure" and the "School of the Nude."[13] Under the master's tutelage Klein developed skill in both life drawing and clay modeling, and, in fact, the high quality of his draughtsmanship and modeling in clay are his finest artistic legacy. An officially stamped letter of recommendation describes Klein as "showing great good will and diligence in the execution of works assigned to him."[14] The letter is signed by the Accademia's President Adolfo Angeli and by Carlo Fontana. This letter of endorsement was probably written at Klein's request in anticipation of his departure for the United States.

By 1928 Carlo Fontana had become the Accademia's most celebrated faculty member attracting students from all over Europe. Fontana's evening courses, such as "the School of the Nude," were especially popular with demand often exceeding available space. Certainly Klein, a foreigner and a trained architect, had to enroll as an irregular student. Given the Accademia's curricular requirements for students in 1928, Klein would have found the regular curriculum in "Architecture and Decoration" redundant of his earlier studies in Ansbach.

Fontana's final full year of teaching at the Accademia was 1928. He left in 1929 following an argument with President Adolfo Angeli over removal of the sculpture teaching studios from the main building. The sculptor Arturo Dazzi took his place.

Fontana's ideological position as an early twentieth century Italian sculptor favored direct experience with materials as opposed to a purely academic and intellectual familiarity favored by many of his contemporaries. This direct approach to materials fostered the honesty found in Klein's most original work.[15]

FIGURE 1

*Josef Klein models an unidentified clay figure at
the Accademia Reale di Belle Arti, Carrara, Italy, 1928.*

FIGURE 2
Klein's first European commission was a marble portrait of Hans Brauns, Imperial Prime Minister of Germany, 1928.

AMERICA: 1928-1930

In the fall of 1928 Klein boarded the steamship *Rama* for America. In the months preceding his departure, as a result of a nationwide competition, Klein won his first important commission to carve in marble a life-size bust of Hans Brauns, Imperial Prime Minister of Germany [fig. 2].[16]

Klein's immigration appears to have been encouraged by two stimuli: work and romance. In Europe he met Mrs. James D. Palmer of Jacksonville, Florida, who soon became his first American patron. Second, his romantic interest in Elizabeth Rimmele, a naturalized German-American citizen, drew him to Miami. They married in 1929. Following his arrival in America and a short stay in New York City, Klein traveled to Jacksonville where he opened his first studio at 2224 Oak Street. Here he completed his first American commission, a portrait sculpture of Mrs. Palmer, a life-size head carved from a block of white Vermont marble.[17]

Through the efforts of his wife-to-be, Klein obtained an important commission from Mrs. Clarence Busch, Elizabeth's employer, who commissioned Klein to do a bust of her daughter Clarice.[18] In Miami Klein completed a self-portrait [fig. 3 and plate 2] and several commissioned portraits of prominent citizens. He also carved a fine granite relief of the German heavyweight boxing champion Max Schmeling [plate 1].[19]

Klein loved stone as an expressive medium. He wrote in an essay titled "A Sculptor,"

The noble and beautiful dwells quite especially in stone which, by a skillful hand, allows itself to be fashioned in the most beautiful and expressive manner. Stone can be worked as to represent the mirror of your soul.[20]

Klein's affection for stone was moderated by the difficulty of obtaining it in Florida. Consequently, after 1929 he turned increasingly to modeling in clay, with later casts in bronze.

In August 1929 Klein married Elizabeth Rimmele in Jacksonville. The couple moved into an apartment at 1502 Dancy Street which also served as Klein's studio. While in Jacksonville Klein exhibited his work at the Casa Marina Hotel, and given his dependence upon sculpture as a source of income, this exhibition in all likelihood was a strictly commercial venture.

Klein occasionally dabbled with painting portraits, even though he possessed little facility for working with oils. In Jacksonville he painted a portrait of President Herbert Hoover, which he offered to sell for ten thousand dollars. This oil painting was a speculative effort made from a photograph supplied to Klein by the White House. According to Klein, the president agreed to sit for his portrait, but cancelled the sitting when a fire in the White House interrupted his routine.[21] Ten years later in 1939, he returned to painting when he believed the possibilities were exhausted for sculptural commissions.[22]

Klein and his wife moved to West Palm Beach in January 1930, remaining there only until March, when they made their way north to Atlanta, Georgia. Here Klein enjoyed his greatest success as a sculptor.

FIGURE 3
In Miami, Klein modeled a terra cotta self-portrait which he later exhibited
in the Atlanta Business and Professional Women's Club "Art-Salon of 1934."

THE ATLANTA YEARS: 1930-1950

In the early spring of 1930 Josef and Elizabeth Klein departed from West Palm Beach on a driving trip that was intended to be a second honeymoon. Their ultimate destination was New York City; however, what was to have been a brief visit in Atlanta became a twenty-year stay. According to a newspaper article Klein described his decision to remain in Atlanta as an accident:

> *We happen to be passing the Studio Arts Building in our automobile and immediately I have a desire to see what is inside. I meet Mrs. Butler, the gracious chatelaine of the colony, and she make us feel so at home that I have a wish to remain for a while in your city.* [23]

Klein's first days in Atlanta were filled with promise. He made new friends, found receptive patrons, and cultivated Atlantans' curiosity about his continental manner and storied past.

THOMAS E. WATSON MEMORIAL

Klein was eager to pursue monumental ideas, and his first opportunity came in 1932 when he won the right to model the bronze figure of Thomas E. Watson, which stands on the grounds of the State Capitol in Atlanta [fig. 4]. Of all the sculptural commissions he was awarded in Atlanta, Klein received the most public praise and attention for the Watson memorial. Thomas E. Watson, United States Senator from Georgia,

FIGURE 4
Klein's bronze statue of Populist Presidential candidate Thomas Watson was his most important Atlanta commission in 1932.

died in office in 1922. He was one of the state's greatest contemporary political figures, an editor, lawyer, historian, author, orator, and statesman. Best known as the presidential nominee of the Populist Party in 1908, Watson served as the congressional author of the U. S. Postal Service's Rural Free Delivery system. Watson obtained a national reputation through the popularity of his three published histories, *The Story of France, Napoleon, Life of Jefferson,* and *Jackson.* He spoke with a fiery oratorical style, which his followers admired and which Klein attempted to incorporate in his concept for the monument.

In 1925 the Thomas Watson Memorial Association began to raise funds in order to erect a statue of the late senator. The association apparently had a difficult time finding the right sculptor for their project. Even after sufficient funds had been raised by popular subscription, the association could not agree upon a sculptor until Klein arrived.[24] In an article in *The City Builder,* Erland W. Bates describes Klein:

> … [a] modern Phidias, who had the touch and understanding of a Michaelangelo…Of all the artists commissioned to submit sketches only Dr. Klein saw the fire and energy of a truly great man looking out of the intense eyes and reflected in the magnificent head of the great Georgian, and thus after a weary world-wide search for an artist to create the memorial, success was found right in America.[25]

In his article Bates makes several references to "Dr. Klein," an appellation that began to appear after "Dr. Joseph Klein" received the degree of Doctor of Natural Science from the American School of Naturopathy in New York City on April 1, 1930.[26] Throughout his Atlanta years, the large, floridly lettered diploma hung neatly framed and prominently displayed on a wall. It seems likely that the "Dr." made Klein seem more important and credible to prospective patrons. In addition Klein changed the spelling of his first name from "Josef" to "Joseph," perhaps because "Joseph" seemed more American to him. Klein usually signed his work "Dr. Joseph Klein"' though he used "Dr. J. Klein," "D. J. K.," and, rarely, "KLEIN." In 1950, when Klein moved from Atlanta to Houston, he again changed his first name, returning to the original "Josef."

Klein's standing figure of Senator Thomas Watson is one and one-half to two times life-size with the final cast bronze figure mounted atop a ten-foot square granite base. The model was prepared first in clay and then a full-scale plaster original was formed and sent to New York, where it was cast. When the casting was complete, it was returned to Klein in Atlanta for final chasing and patination.

Governor Richard B. Russell offered any spot within the capitol building or on the capitol grounds for the placement of the sculpture. Klein and a committee consisting of James H. Boykin, chair of the Watson Memorial Association; John I. Kelley, assistant attorney general; J. J. Flynt, judge; Benjamin Blackburn and R. S. Steele of Atlanta selected a site for the sculpture on the Washington Street plaza section of the capitol grounds.[27]

The unveiling of the Watson monument took place in a ceremony on the state capitol grounds, Saturday, December 3, 1932.[28] The *Atlanta Journal* provided front-page, illustrated coverage of the event. As many as three thousand people listened to addresses from Georgia's Governor-elect Eugene Herman Talmadge, and Senators Walter F. George of Georgia and Thomas F. Heflin of Alabama. Although Klein did not speak at the unveiling, he was prominently photographed alongside Watson family members and Senators George and Heflin.[29]

Klein's conception for the Watson figure was not without its detractors. Watson is modeled striding boldly forward with his left arm raised, elbow bent, and fist tightly clenched. The figure is mobile and aggressive. While everyone who cared to express an opinion in print agreed that Watson was a combative, dynamic presence in life, a debate erupted over Watson's right or left-handedness.[30] Critics claimed that because of the raised fist, Klein depicted Watson as being left-handed. Close friends of Watson's confirmed the late senator's left-handedness. Others, including Watson's biographer, used the dexterity issue as a pretext to criticize the statue's placement on the capitol grounds; they believed it was too dominating, placed as it was symmetrically centered before the capitol building directly across the street from the historic Central Presbyterian Church.

MONUMENT TO LABOR PROPOSAL

In 1933, following closely on the heels of his triumph as the sculptor of the Watson Memorial, Klein proposed construction of a "great monument to labor." He hoped the city of Atlanta would sponsor this project, but there was little interest and no funding. Klein described his idea in a letter to James L. Key, Mayor of Atlanta.[31] The letter opens with a long, rambling, negative assessment of cultural life in Atlanta, followed by his proposal.

> *Very recently I have come to the idea, whether it would be possible through your cooperation to build a statue to labor and have it put up in Piedmont Park, about 25 to 30 feet high, in artificial reinforced stone…I already started a study, about 2 feet high, a single man, in a very natural pose, representing simplicity and the spirit of our present day laborer. To my estimation such a monument would be a great honor and encouragement to the average man who deserves to be symbolized while he cuts his bread alive. From another viewpoint, I believe such a statue will create…interest and eventually national reputation, and be for Atlanta of great value in many respects.* [32]

The study Klein describes is made of terra cotta with a very light grey patina to simulate the color and texture of the artificial stone he hoped to use for his monument [plate 25]. There is no record of Mayor Key's response to Klein's letter or of any support offered for the proposal for the monument to labor.

JOEL CHANDLER HARRIS

Controversy was not new to Klein, and in 1934 his involvement with a planned memorial to Joel Chandler Harris created a controversy from which his sculptural career never recovered. Dr. M. L. Brittain, president of Georgia Institute of Technology, and Colonel Frederic J. Paxon, chairman of the Uncle Remus Memorial Association, wanted to erect a memorial to Joel Chandler Harris, creator of the Uncle Remus tales and a native Georgian.[33] It is difficult to say who originated the idea for a sculptural memorial to Joel Chandler Harris, but it was Josef Klein who first translated their idea into a practical concept and visual form. At first, everyone rallied around Klein's proposal for the monument. He was enthusiastically backed by the Uncle Remus Memorial Association, the Harris family, and leading citizens of the state, including Colonel Sam Tate and Clark Howell, publisher of the *Atlanta Constitution*.[34]

Initial enthusiasm for the Harris project quickly turned into a plan of action for raising the necessary funds to construct the monument. Dr. Brittain conceived the idea of using a radio campaign to solicit money from the public to build the monument. Colonel Tate donated twenty-five thousand dollars' worth of Georgia marble from which the monument was to be carved, and Howell offered liberal space in his newspaper for coverage of the fund-raising campaign.

A written description, in Klein's own hand, outlines his plan for the monument. His preliminary drawings for the monument [plates 38 and 39] seem to vary little from this description:

> The Uncle Remus memorial is to be erected in marble with the exception of the animal characters and the negro figure which will be cast in bronze. The statue of Joel Chandler Harris will reach a height of 16 to 18 feet and the boy and the negro 1/3 over life size. The whole monument will be 28 or 30 feet in height. The principal figure, J. C. Harris, clad in a toga, represents the finished student, scholar, lawyer and poet. The bowl he is holding in his right hand is a symbol of generosity, for with his stories he has filled many youthful hearts with joy and happiness…The base is holding 8 reliefs, the most outstanding characters of his stories…The work as a whole is a symbol of the south. [35]

Klein allowed his design for the memorial to be published and widely disseminated around the country. He even mailed a copy of the design to the Accademia Reale di Belle Arti in Carrara, Italy. *Time* magazine, in a telegram, questioned Klein's draping of Joel Chandler Harris in a robe. Klein explained that the robe is a "symbol of dignity, of law, of scholarship." [36] Though he favored depicting Harris wearing a broad-brimmed hat, Klein created a hatless alternative drawing [plate 38].

The radio campaign for the memorial fund was sponsored by Atlanta radio station WGST, which operated under the auspices of the Georgia Institute of Technology. It was President Brittain's goal to raise one hundred thousand dollars by broadcasting appeals to the general public for subscriptions to the memorial fund. Everything seemed to be in place to assure successful fundraising. Klein had the backing of the Harris family, the memorial association, the *Atlanta Constitution*, and powerful individual backers. But, the unanimity did not last, because no one involved in planning the project considered the wishes of the Artists' Guild of Atlanta.

Even as funds for the project were being solicited, the Artists' Guild issued a statement protesting the erection of the Harris Memorial without first staging an open competition. The *Atlanta Constitution* published the complete text of the guild's statement:

> The Artists' Guild of Atlanta,…protested against the awarding of public art projects paid for by funds solicited from the public at large without supervision by some group or commission and without the usual competitive form.
> The guild sincerely approves of an appropriate memorial to the beloved writer, but insists that the design for such a memorial should be selected in such a way as to insure the public that it be the best obtainable. They, therefore, recommend that the sculptor should be selected by means of an open competition properly supervised by the Atlanta Art Commission, a group of five men annually appointed by the mayor, or some other representative organization. [37]

As soon as the Artists' Guild's letter was published, the Harris family expressed reservations about proceeding with the project as planned. Joel Chandler Harris Jr. and his brother Evelyn acquiesced to the guild's demands for a design competition. Plans which had been rapidly moving forward were put on hold while guidelines for a competition were hurriedly drawn up. The award of the commission, which had been a certainty for Klein, was now in doubt.

Klein violently opposed the idea of an open design competition, and made his hostility known to the Harris family. In a letter to the "Honorable Harris Family," Klein wrote:

In reference to the idea of competition I desire to state the follow-ing: The greatest pieces of sculpture the world has brought forth by genius are a matter of non-competition, as competition destroys the pride of a genius and is against his fundamental rule and sinceri-ty and if these facts are handicapped, the work will take the aspect of mediocrity. Men of great self-confidence and power shall accept constructive criticism, but shall not be guided by committees or indi-viduals, who have not tasted the struggle of a sculptor who is sin-cere with himself and his environment. Michelangelo has received his commissions without competition, but on merit. Rodin has made his greatest masterpiece of Balzac without competition. [38]

In another letter to Joel Chandler Harris Jr. Klein goes even further in his antagonism.

Your brother Evelyn wrote to me a friendly letter recently that he is still of the opinion to have this memorial done on a competitive basis. Of course, if the family is insisting on that I shall withdraw from the activities and interest I have taken in his matter. Compe-titions are only for students and beginners and if the people of Geor-gia would have no confidence in me, I would be much better off to settle in another state. [39]

Despite the blustering, threatening tone, Klein's argument against a competition had merit. He had been publicly recognized as the sculp-tor of the Harris Memorial; he had allowed "thousands of letters and pho-tographs of the proposed memorial to be sent out all over the U. S...," [40] and he believed, perhaps correctly, that this broad exposure of his plan would give competitors an unfair advantage.

Klein became so distraught over the untoward turn of events that he threatened, in a letter to his lawyer, to bring a a half-million dollar law-suit against the Harris family. [41] The suit was never more than a threat, but Klein's vituperation seems to have had its desired effect, if Klein could not prevail in the matter of a competition, neither he nor anyone should build the memorial. Consequently, the drive to raise funds and all activ-ities related to the planned project were abandoned. While he was able to derail this popular project it was ultimately a hollow victory, because Klein never again won the backing of Atlanta's business and cultural lead-ers for a large-scale sculptural project.

THE GIGANTIC HEAD OF CHRIST

The Joel Chandler Harris fiasco was not Klein's last attempt to achieve sculptural immortality. He made a final venture into monumental sculp-ture between 1936 and 1939. Working in a garage-workshop at 1009 Colum-bia Avenue, Klein modeled and carved an eight-foot head of Christ. This huge work, constructed of more than one ton of plaster, was to embody the idea of "victory through defeat." [42]

Klein's head was a solitary effort, conceived as a purely speculative venture. He had neither financial backing nor public support for this project, but he had a clear end in mind for his work. He designed the eight-foot head as a scale model for a much larger work, which he envi-sioned at a height of thirty feet. This heroic effort was to be carved of marble or granite and placed on a wooded hilltop, near a highway, some-where in Georgia {plate 47].

The massive eight-foot plaster model was the largest work Klein ever attempted. With the help of ten men, he moved his sculpture to Atlanta's City Auditorium in 1939 where it was mounted on a nine-foot pedestal as a backdrop for a meeting of the Baptist World Alliance. In preparation for the meeting Klein manufactured a number of small plaster models, presumably to sell as souvenirs of the conference [plate 34]. Klein never realized his plan to enlarge this sculpture, and, in 1950, when he moved his family to Houston, he left behind the gigantic head of Christ. If the sculpture exists today, its whereabouts is unknown.

In one newspaper account describing Klein's grandiose plans for his head of Christ, the family's impoverishment is also mentioned. The anonymous writer describes how Klein completed a landscape painting which he traded to his milkman for an order of one hundred dollars' worth of milk to be delivered two quarts daily until the order ran out.[43] Later, describing her family's financial circumstances during the Atlanta years, Klein's daughter uses the phrase "feast or famine." When the sculptor fulfilled a commission, the family ate well and lived in relative peace; when there was no work, the family struggled for subsistence. One clear indicator of the family's struggle to survive is preserved in eviction notices served on Klein in 1937, 1938, 1939 and 1942.[44]

OTHER RELIGIOUS WORKS

Was Josef Klein a religious man? And, occurring as it did near the end of his sculptural career (1939), did Klein's head of Christ signal some sort of a religious conversion? The answer to both of these questions is "no." According to his family, Klein had no conventional religious convictions. He did, however, allow himself to get as near religion as a reading of Friedrich Nietzsche permitted.[45]

The head of Christ was one of Klein's last Atlanta sculptures. It is revealing to look back at several pieces completed between 1930 and 1934. His 1933 *Hand from the Cross* [plate 29] is expressively modeled. This clay hand desperately grips the earth from which it was formed, the same earth from which Jehovah fashioned Adam. Sinew and bone are flexed and taut. A gaping spike wound in the back of the hand seems to implicate each viewer in the suffering of the crucifixion. Were Matthias Grunewald a sculptor he might have fashioned a similarly compelling expression of pain.

Although it is abstract, *Trinitas* [plate 22] is clearly a stylized interpretation of the Holy Trinity. Angular planes of three elongated faces simultaneously merge into a modern iconic form. When the Business and Professional Women's Club of Atlanta invited Klein to exhibit his work in the "Art-Salon of 1934," a photograph of *Trinitas* was chosen for the cover of the exhibition catalogue. Klein liked this sculpture so well that he later used it as the logo identifying his Houston design firm.

The most striking example of Klein's expressive modeling is his *Croce di Guerra* [fig. 5], which was part of Georgia's state exhibition at the Chicago World's Fair in 1933. Ten of Klein's sculptures were selected for the Fair by the Georgia Century of Progress Commission, and press coverage of the Georgia Exhibition centered on Klein; other contributors, if there were any, were not mentioned in the press. *Croce di Guerra*, a life-size plaster study shows a World War I soldier crucified on a cross and a dollar sign, a part of one arm blown away, one leg drawn in pain, and the other pulling away from this crucifix. A Chicago newspaper reviewer commented that, "…the idea that war is an unsuccessful commercial proposition because of the sacrifice of manhood is given to the viewer. The work is attracting particular attention because of the emotions expressed in the face and body of the figure."[46] *Croce di Guerra* is essentially moralizing in tone. Klein believed in the power of sculpture to change society, and he wanted to lead the way with his work. He saw his sculpture as an ethical corrective which could alter society's misguided "worship" of money. This idealistic attitude was somewhat mitigated by Klein's dependence upon Atlanta's moneyed interests for his own survival.

A propensity to exhort is further evident in Klein's semi-abstract *Selfish Epoch* [plate 21]. A gaunt face is architectonically combined with a cross, a heart, a dollar sign, a quartered section of a female breast, and

FIGURE 5
Croce di Guerra *was one of Klein's ten sculptured contributions to the Chicago World's Fair in 1933.*

a hand holding a dangling cigarette. The heart, usually a symbol of charity, in *Selfish Epoch* is firmly "branded" with a dollar sign. Klein's juxtaposing of these symbols against a geometric framework presumably defines his vision of a self-indulgent age as seen by the artist from his perspective during the Depression.

THE PORTRAITS

Klein had already completed portrait commissions in Jacksonville and Miami by the time he moved to Atlanta in 1930. He wasted no time arranging a one-man exhibition for himself at the High Museum of Art, then located in the Joseph M. High house at 1262 Peachtree Street. Details of how this exhibition was arranged are unavailable but it is likely Klein acted on his own behalf in approaching the director. The museum, still in its infancy, having only been established in 1926, may have been pleased to offer exhibition space to "one of the outstanding young sculptors of the present time…"[47] In this exhibition Klein showcased his talent for portraiture by exhibiting, among other works, his carved marble bust of Mrs. James D. Palmer of Jacksonville and a terra cotta *Self Portrait* [plate 2]. Lewis Palmer Skidmore, director of the High Museum, commented on Klein's "unusually fine modern handling" of bas relief in *The Foul Blow* and in a life-size figure, *The Awakening of Youth*.[48] In conjunction with the High Museum's exhibition, Klein modeled in clay a bust of the director's daughter, twelve-year-old Ann Skidmore (fig. 6). Later, the bust was completed and displayed at the museum.

Klein's first opportunity for an important portrait commission in Atlanta came from the Atlanta Women's Club in the fall of 1931. He was asked to model a bust of Enrico Leide, cellist and long-time Atlanta symphony conductor. The unveiling of the bust at the Fox Theater was reported as a major cultural event. More than three thousand spectators turned out for the unveiling and a performance by a sixty-piece orchestra. Klein figured prominently in the activities, using his moment in the limelight to call for "an awakening of interest in art and in sculpture particularly."[49]

During the years that followed, Klein completed a number of important portraits of prominent Georgians. The most important, in addition to the Leide bust, are: Clark Howell [fig. 7], publisher of the *Atlanta Constitution* (1932); Dr. Claude N. Hughes, dentist and philanthropist (1932); Lionel H. Keene, southern division manager of Lowes, Inc. (1932); James L. Key, mayor of Atlanta (1932-33); Eugene Herman Talmadge, governor of Georgia (1933); Frank L. Stanton [plate 32], first poet laureate of Georgia (1935); Eugene R. Black, governor of the Federal Reserve Board (1936); James L. Mayson, city attorney, Atlanta (1936); William Berry Hartsfield, mayor of Atlanta (1937); Arthur Brisbane, editor and columnist (1939); Columbus Roberts, state commissioner of agriculture (1939).

While Klein thrived as a portrait sculptor, his most expressive and creative portraits were those inspired by famous people, about whom he had often only read. Working exclusively from newspaper photographs or book plates, he created several of his most striking portraits, such as those of Thomas Alva Edison [plate 23] and Robert E. Lee [plate 10]. Shortly after Thomas Edison's death in 1931, Klein began work on an impressive life-size terra cotta bust.

Curiously, several of Klein's portraits are clearly caricatures. Most notable is his satirical portrait of governor Eugene Herman Talmadge [fig. 8]. The Governor is sculpted as a laughing, demented bumpkin who bears a striking resemblance to Franklin D. Roosevelt. In newspaper interviews Klein described Talmadge as a fascinating character whom he admired.[50] It seems likely that Klein objected to Talmadge neither personally nor politically, and that the sculpture was a jest. Apparently, Talmadge did not take offense at Klein's caricature because he granted permission for photographs of the sculpture to be published.[51] Klein, who had affection for neither Fascism or Nazism, sculpted Benito Mus-

FIGURE 6
In this 1930 photograph, Klein models a portrait of Ann Skidmore, daughter of the High Museum's director.

FIGURE 7
Klein contemplates his bust of Clark Howell, publisher of the Atlanta Constitution.

FIGURE 8

A photograph of Klein's modeled caricature of Governor Eugene Herman Talmadge (1933) received wide circulation in the Atlanta Journal.

solini as a sneering dictator [plate 9], and the features of Adolph Hitler [plate 7] are distorted and angry. Wiley Post's exaggerated features and lopsided grin accentuate his swashbuckling reputation [plate 8]. Klein's respect for the role of caricature in art is evident in a fragmentary passage written by him in Atlanta.

Many people regard it (caricature) as somewhat trivial and insignificant art. They say it is comic. Yet caricature has been universal. Certain early Chinese paintings may be regarded as religious caricatures with serious and elevated pretensions. Daumier used it frequently to express a deadly earnestness of moral indignation. The art of caricature then forces us to admit that drawing can…handle the same stuff as literature, can model psychological phenomena. [52]

THEMATIC WORKS

Klein was able to work most freely and without pretention when he worked for private, purely aesthetic reasons. He worked spontaneously and unselfconsciously with traditional secular themes such as the male and female nude, the mother and child, wrestlers, dancers, and romantic couples. These sculptures, usually diminutive, were created without concern for their marketability, although Klein exhibited them during the 1930s. After 1945, Klein ceased creating or publically exhibiting these works, which he never sold.

Klein's *Slave* [plate 20], created in time for the Atlanta Business and Professional Women's *Art-Salon of 1934,* is a remarkable allegory of escape and hard-won freedom. Although it is small (12½ inches in height), it may be Klein's finest achievement. His *Slave* looks back, fear and tension clearly mirrored in the modeling of the face and figure. The clay from which *Slave* is modeled becomes a metaphor of the struggle to break free of the servitude that shackled an entire race. An image of such strength and character, created in the heart of a segregated South during the 1930s, is remarkable, but perhaps Klein's *Slave* seems more extraordinary in retrospect than it did when it was first exhibited. Although photographs of five of Klein's sculptures were reproduced in the *Art-Salon* exhibition catalogue, *Slave* appears only as a title on the exhibition checklist, and it was never singled out by reviewers for comment. As an immigrant, Klein was sensitive to the scourge of racial prejudice, and during World War II he and his family would suffer tangibly from the widespread anti-German sentiment which swept across America.

Klein loved to work out-of-doors. In the early 1930s, passersby often glimpsed him working at the Grant Park Zoo. *Monkey* (*the Thinker*) [plate 24] is an arresting figure modeled in clay near the monkey cages. The sculpture is lifelike, sentient, even soulful, and seems more human than not. While the title *Monkey* is factually descriptive of his subject, it is the subtitle (*the Thinker*) which qualifies Klein's objective in creating the work. He takes the vague self-recognition zoo-goers commonly admit at the monkey cages and heightens it, making it tangible and personal.

ATLANTA'S CULTURAL CLIMATE: THE 1930S

Walter C. Hill, writing in his unpublished "History of Art in Atlanta of 1941," paraphrases H.L. Mencken in referring to the city as the "Sahara of American Art."[53] This phrase symbolized for Hill the negative perceptions of cultural development in Atlanta during the first four decades of the twentieth century. When Josef Klein arrived in 1930, the Atlanta Art Association had just established the city's first art museum and school of art. Even though Atlantans traveled to Europe, supported annual Metropolitan Opera concerts, built large homes, and collected art, there is no evidence of important philanthropy until 1926 when Mrs. Joseph M. High presented her former home to the Atlanta Art Association to be used as a permanent museum of art for the city.[54] While Mrs. High's gift was a generous one, Atlanta's cultural support lagged far behind other southern cities. Charleston, South Carolina, with its Gibbes Gallery (established in 1858) had long been a cultural center. Memphis, Tennessee, had an art museum by 1916 (the Brooks), and Savannah's Telfair Academy of Arts and Sciences opened in 1886.

Atlanta's vigorous material and commercial growth continued well into the 1930s but was not accompanied by corresponding cultural growth. Arts organizations had shaky economic foundations and garnered little encouragement from city government. Josef Klein individually managed to do what every arts organization found difficult if not impossible; he attracted patronage from business and civic leaders. Atlanta's newspapers were generally supportive of the arts community and "promoted the attendance of art exhibitions so…the city would become enlightened to aesthetics, thereby raising its status in the eyes of more established cities of the North."[55] Newspaper editors gave Klein's exhibitions and commissions generous coverage.

ATLANTA: THE 1940S

For economic reasons, late in the 1930s and throughout the 1940s Klein shifted some of his emphasis from sculpture to painting and interior design. He wrote about his shift from sculpture to painting in 1939:

At this juncture, I felt that my enthusiasm was partly exhausted in the matter of clay. Good fortune, however, was on my side and orders for [painted] portraits came in abundance and these brought fairly good prices, enabling me to live in more tranquility of mind than in previous years. To date, I have executed portraits of many prominent ladies and gentlemen. I might say that some of these portraits are good, some bad, and others only indifferent. [56]

The quality of his painted portraits may have been questionable, but because of his success as a sculptor Klein's Atlanta patrons came to trust his painting. It is an anomalous quality of Klein's talent that he consistently drew portraits in pencil with great skill and sensitivity but could only occasionally translate that sensitivity into paint. Klein's sculptural portraits in terra cotta, like his drawings, were consistently sensitive and expressive.

Probably a combination of hubris, poverty, and the deprivation of the war years effectively ended Klein's career as a sculptor. As the sole breadwinner for his family (his wife did not work outside the home) Klein felt at times overwhelmed by circumstances. Commenting on his family's misery in 1941, Klein wrote,

For a large part we lived on bread. For vegetables we had dandelion mixed with lettuce. Meat dishes were scanty, but fortunately we did have milk for the children. Like burning embers mysterious days rushed at us, and I can only attribute it to my will, which kept me from despairing completely. There I stood as though no other person could understand my thoughts. My depictions in my work just stood there, without fulfilling any hope. What use is a noble opinion if one lives among human wolves, whose teeth tear up the flesh of the ideal leaving its spirit wanting. It was no longer only a question of creating works of art, but to create sustenance for four mouths…[57]

Klein's despair was profound. He could not work, and after Germany's declaration of war on America, his German citizenship became a liability. Writing just after Japan's attack on Pearl Harbor, he said,

Germany followed with a declaration of war, which was to be expected. All these circumstances contributed to obscuring my outlook, especially since I was conscious of being a foreigner. The following day already the newspaper headlines announced the arrest of several Germans. [58]

Klein was haunted by the fear that he would be arrested because he owned photographic equipment and a short-wave radio. At this time, ownership of these ordinary devices was pretext enough for a charge of treason to be brought against the owner, if that person were not an American citizen. Klein knew the risk he was taking by retaining possession of this equipment.

Foreigners were not allowed to have radios and cameras. But I myself risked the danger of hanging on to my two short-wave radios and also my cameras. The main reason was my poverty, since I counted on selling these things if the opportunity ever presented itself in order to take care of my needs. For if I had handed them over to the police I would not have gotten anything. Moreover, it was very hard for me to give up my cameras. A camera is a thing one holds dear, and then I took pictures of my pieces, if not just for the love of it but also to have a record of the finished pieces. [59]

Klein had a premonition that one day a knock would come at his door, and he would be arrested.

I always had the feeling, — that my hour would come when the gentlemen of the secret police would lay their hands on me. Not that I was hiding anything in my conscience that the world could not know. My understanding and thinking would never burden my mind with the knowledge of harming my authorities or my fellow man. Not for money and not for material things. [60]

The fateful day of his arrest finally came in 1942. Klein's youngest child, Siegfried, clearly remembers the FBI's "visit" and offers the following account of his father's arrest. Siegfried was eight years old at the time of his father's detention:

Two men walked up to the house. They asked me if I knew Dr. Joseph Klein. I told them he was my father. They then asked me if my father liked Adolph Hitler. I innocently answered, "Yes," knowing only that he was German and also that my father had modeled a likeness of Hitler in clay. The two agents searched the house, seized my father's cameras and other photographic equipment and left. The next day they returned carrying some papers; they arrested my father, leading him away from our house in handcuffs. I cried while hanging onto his pants leg. For a long time I blamed myself for his arrest. [61]

Klein was taken to the federal detention center at Fort McPherson, just outside Atlanta. He remained at Fort McPherson for six months, until he was cleared of suspicion that he was a spy. While there, Klein was allowed to use pencils and paper for drawing, he sketched portraits of his fellow detainees, [plate 49] and also drew romantic fantasies of nude female figures [plates 50 and 51]. These sketches are bold and direct. Women in all of Klein's drawings and sculptures are depicted as vigorous; they are healthy, active creatures.

In 1944 Klein opened what the *Atlanta Constitution* called "Atlanta's first independent art gallery." [62] With this gallery, located at 149 North Avenue near Piedmont, Klein intended to feature his own work. The newspaper account of the gallery's opening makes no mention of any interest in the work of artists other than himself. The article primarily has Klein discussing his painting, and, curiously, his sculpture seems almost incidental to the feature. By this time Klein refers to himself as an artist, a designer, and a creator, not as a sculptor. The gallery was a temporary, not very successful venture according to his childrens' recollection.

The only record of his artistic activity in 1945 is an announcement of his participating in a group painting exhibition at George Chapellier Gallery in New York City. Along with Robert Philipp, Robert Brackman, Jon Corbino, Ernest Lawson, Louis Bosa, E. Chocke, and Otto Biernals, Klein exhibited eight to ten still life paintings.[63] Details of the exhibition's content or of Klein's participation are not included in the *Atlanta Constitution's* report.

In 1950 the Klein family moved to Houston where Josef owned and operated a cabinet shop, featuring custom furniture design and construction and interior decoration services. Klein dropped the "Dr." from his name and returned to the original spelling of his first name "Josef."[64]

HOUSTON: 1950 - 1992

Klein hoped to revive his artistic career in Houston and make money in the process. He reasoned that the city's thriving business climate would welcome his art. However, as in Atlanta, the presence of an active successful business community did not automatically translate into an active interest in high culture, and Klein found the initial going difficult.

In a *Houston Post* feature, Klein described himself as a student of French impressionism and an expressionistic portrait painter. He rather combatively explained that his expressionistic approach to portraiture is art while other more realistic approaches are not. He stated that he will only accept a portrait commission if he can paint it his way.[65]

Klein's studio in Houston was located on Louisiana Street near his family's apartment, owned by Houston decorator Parker Edwards. Edwards was Klein's first important contact in Houston, and became a friend and mentor. Klein learned the decorating business from Edwards, and eventually started a firm of his own located in Houston's Riverside area. He later relocated to River Oaks where he lived within walking distance of his shop. While there was little demand for Klein's expressionistic portraiture, orders for his built-in cabinets and furniture designs were steady.

Despite the success of his business, Klein was not a good manager of money or people. He refused to pay bills on time, and his fits of anger threatened to ruin the business when he drove potential customers away by insulting their taste and insisting that he knew best their furniture and decorating needs. His wife Elizabeth, and his children became increasingly involved in the day-to-day operation of the business, and Klein withdrew from the business and from the world. After several years of living in virtual seclusion, and following a brief illness, Josef Klein died in Houston on June 9, 1992.

CONCLUSION

A visit to the site of the Thomas Watson memorial on the grounds of Georgia's capitol affirms what is best in Josef Klein's art. Crowds of school children and other visitors to the capitol most often gather at the granite base of the monument for photographs. The figure's placement is picturesque and dominant, symmetrically centered before the gold-domed capitol building. Watson looks directly across Washington Street at the historic Central Presbyterian Church.

When the Watson statue was erected in 1932, the only sculpture in place on the capitol grounds were two Confederate memorials. One of these, a bronze equestrian figure of General John Brown Gordon, still faces the junction of Martin Luther King Avenue and Washington Street. The other Civil War memorial, a seated statue of Georgia's Civil War Governor, Joseph Emerson Brown and his wife Elizabeth Grisham Brown, occupies the corner of Mitchell Avenue and Washington Street. Klein's sculpture including its base rises to seventeen feet in height. Its scale, placement and dramatic pose secure the Watson figure's visual dominance of the grounds despite the addition in recent years of two other bronzes nearby. The closest "competitor" for the visitor's attention is William Thompson's figure of Richard Russell. Russell's figure is actually larger than Watson's but is so poorly placed that its visual appeal is compromised, especially with its flat, unheroic base.

In 1994 a bronze monument to James Earl Carter Jr. was placed almost against the capitol's looming lower facade. Frederick E. Hart depicts Carter as exactly life-size, mounted on a minimal base located almost at ground level. The scale seems apologetic and overly modest, and the figure's balance is troublesome, swaying forward from the hips in an almost drunken stance.

Klein's figure of Thomas Watson is unapologetic and credible, possessing a vitality that successfully challenges its successors. It conveys a pugnacious self-confidence that reportedly characterized Watson in life. The figure's active pose and scale command our attention, so that more than sixty years after its creation visitors to the capitol still stop, look, and admire it.

Through his sculpture, especially the portraits, Klein expresses those qualities which serve to ennoble and dignify humanity. For Klein, creating art was an act of moral responsibility. On a scrap of paper he jotted this note: "A great many people…regard art as a luxury. But may I say that this is not so. Art has a very practical side and a stupendous one. Art is the builder of character; on the other hand it takes character to build it."

Klein's work is a dramatic testimony to the all too often obscured contributions of immigrant artists living and working in America during the early part of the twentieth century. This essay and the Georgia Museum of Art's exhibition represents the first in-depth look at the contribution of Josef Klein to the cultural heritage of Atlanta and Georgia. It is hoped that this study challenges misconceptions about, and excites interest in the art of other forgotten immigrants.

WILLIAM T. SQUIRES

NOTES

1. Josef Klein, "Paris, 7 April 1927" (Typescript in German, translated by Barbara Cooper, property of Gloria Frame, executor of Klein's estate, henceforth referred to as Klein estate, Houston), 1.

2. *Ibid.*, 2-3.

3. *Ibid.*, 24-25.

4. *Ibid.*, 2.

5. *Ibid.*, 19.

6. *Ibid.*, 20-21.

7. "Sculptor, Once Driven from Italy by Fascisti, Now Here to Model in Peace," *Palm Beach Post,* 9 January 1930, 1.

8. Joseph Klein, "Biographical Sketch" (Typescript in English, Atlanta, Georgia) Klein estate, 1.

9. Report, Private Training Classes for Workers in the Building Trade by Architect Hans Grauf (Ansbach, Bavaria, 25 April 1924), unpaginated.

10. *Ibid.*, 5.

11. Borromei to Josef Klein, 21 September 1926, Milan, and Davide to Klein, 4 April 1926, Genoa. Klein estate.

12. Klein, "Biographical Skietch," 1.

13. Letter of recommendation, Accademia Reale di Belle Arti by Adolfo Angeli and Carlo Fontana (Carrara, 31 May 1928) Klein estate.

14. *Ibid.*

15. Luigi Servolini, *Carlo Fontana, Scultore 1865-1956* (Carrara: Grafiche Sarzanesi, 1973) 13.

16. "Sculptor, . . ." *Palm Beach Post,* 9 January 1930.

17. "Sculptor Once Driven Out of Italy by Mussolini Now Lives Here; Looks to Hoover Sitting," *Florida Times Union,* 24 November 1928, 1.

18. *Ibid.*

19. "Walked 2,600 Miles for Art," *Atlanta Journal,* 20 April 1930, 10.

20. Joseph Klein, "A Sculptor" (Handwritten manuscript, 1929-30) Klein estate, unpaginated.

21. "Walked 2,600 Miles . . ." *Atlanta Journal,* 10.

22. Klein, "Biographical Sketch," 2.

23. "Walked 2,600 Miles . . ." *Atlanta Journal,* 10.

24. E. W. Bates, "Famous Sculptor Finishes Watson Statue," *The City Builder,* December 1932, 8.

25. *Ibid.*

26. The American School of Naturopathy was founded September 15, 1896 by Benedict Lust, N. D. and M. D. The school was incorporated by the State of New York in 1905.

27. "Sites at Capitol Being Considered For Watson Statue," *Atlanta Journal,* 5 October 1932, 1.

28. "Thousands Pay Tribute to Tom Watson as Statue Is Unveiled on Capitol Lawn," *Atlanta Journal,* 4 December 1932, 1.

29. *Ibid.*

30. "Tom Watson Left-Handed His Statue Is," *Atlanta Constitution,* 13 March 1940, 1.

31. Klein to Key, 31 October 1933, Atlanta, unpaginated.

32. *Ibid.*

33. "Drive to be Launched for Harris Memorial," *Atlanta Constitution,* 7 August 1934, 1.

34 "WGST Sponsor of Campaign for $100, 000," *Atlanta Georgian*, 8 August 1934, 1.

35 Undated handwritten manuscript page by Klein.

36 Klein to J. C. Harris, Jr. , Atlanta, unpaginated.

37 "Harris Memorial Plans Protested By Artists' Guild," *Atlanta Journal*, 12 August 1934, 1.

38 Klein to Harris Family, Altanta, unpaginated.

39 Klein to J. C. Harris, Jr. , Atlanta, unpaginated.

40 *Ibid.*

41 Klein to Calhoun, Atlanta, unpaginated.

42 "Modernistic Conception of Christ Made in Statue Eight Feet High," *Atlanta Constitution*, 12 September 1937, 10.

43 *Ibid.*

44 Municipal Court of Atlanta, Dispossessory Warrant No. 136623 and Warrant No. 159808, The Maccabees vs. Klein, 5 August 1937, and 26 September 1938, Civil Court of Fulton County, Dispossessory Warrant No. 8879, Mrs. S. H. Carter Estate vs. Klein, 7 July 1939. Civil Court of Fulton County, Dispossessory Warrant No. 74351, Mission Board of the Methodist Church vs. Klein, 30 November 1942.

45 Interview with Gloria Frame, Houston, 16 January 1993.

46 "Hailed at Fair," *Atlanta Constitution*, 8 July 1933, 1.

47 "German Sculptor will do Life Size Statue of Ed Hamm," *Atlanta Journal*, 14 April 1930, 1.

48 "Modern Sculptural Exhibit On View Now at Art Museum," *Atlanta Constitution*, 23 October 1930, 2.

49 "3, 000 See Bust of Leide Presented at Concert," *Atlanta Georgian*, 12 October 1931, 1.

50 "Klein Will Paint If He Can Do It His Way," *Houston Post*, 30 April 1950.

51 "Georgia's Governor as a Sculptor Sees Him," *Atlanta Journal*, 24 September 1933, rotogravure section, unpaginated.

52 Klein, "A Sculptor," unpaginated.

53 Walter C. Hill, "History of Art in Atlanta," 1941 (Typescript, Atlanta Historical Society), 119.

54 Carlyn G. Crannell, "In Pursuit of Culture: A History of Art Activity in Atlanta, 1847-1926" (Ph. D. diss. , Emory University, 1981), 340.

55 *Ibid.* vi.

56 Klein, "Biographical Sketch," 2.

57 Josef Klein, (Typescript in German, Atlanta, 1941) Klein estate, unpaginated.

58 *Ibid.*

59 *Ibid.*

60 *Ibid.*

61 Interview with Siegfried Joseph Klein, Houston, 16 January 1993.

62 "Dr. Joseph Klein Opens Independent Art Gallery," *Atlanta Constitution*, 26 November 1944, 8.

63 "Joseph Klein Paintings Win New Honors," *Atlanta Constitution*, 4 November 1945, 16.

64 "Klein Will Paint…," *Houston Post*, 30 April 1950, 2.

65 *Ibid.*

CATALOGUE
OF THE EXHIBITION

All sculptures are listed first, then drawings. Only the height of sculpture is listed. A drawing's height precedes width. All the works in this exhibition are the property of the estate of Josef Klein.

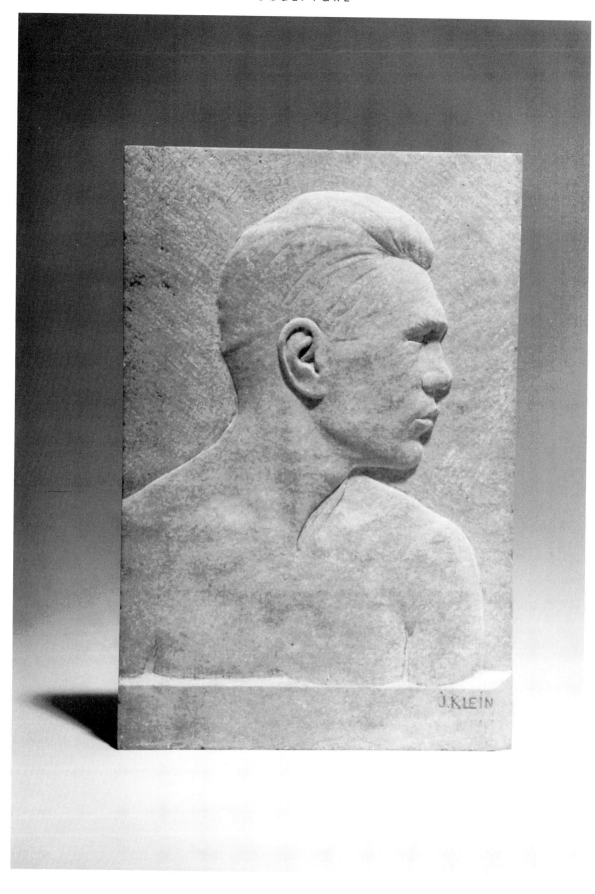

1. *Max Schmeling*
  c. 1929
  Carved granite relief
  11⅝ inches

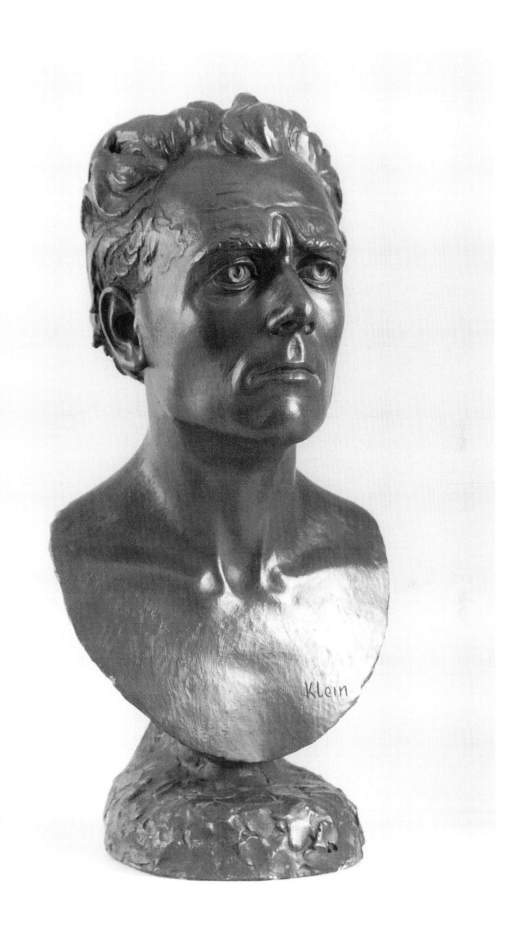

2. *Self-Portrait*
   1929 - 30
   Terra cotta
   21½ inches

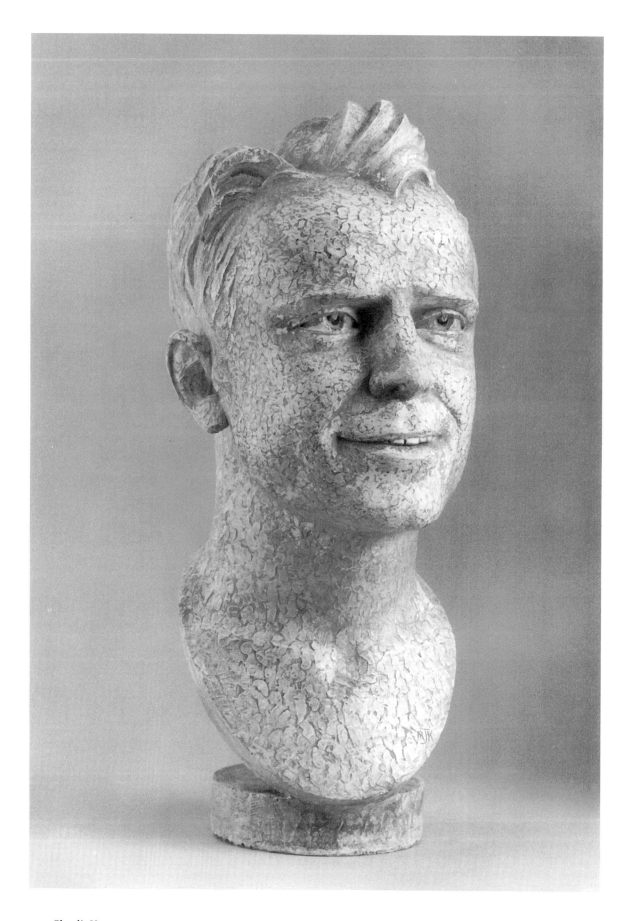

3. *Charlie Yates*
   1930
   Plaster
   20 ½ inches

4. *NIRA* (National Industrial Recovery Act)
1930 - 34
Terra cotta
22 ½ inches

5. *Gloria*
   1930 - 34
   Cast brass and bronze
   11½ inches

6. *Head of Lola, the Dancer*
1930 - 34
Cast bronze
19 inches

7. *Hitler*
   1930 - 34
   Terra cotta
   12 inches

8. *Wiley Post*
1930 - 34
Terra cotta
9 ½ inches

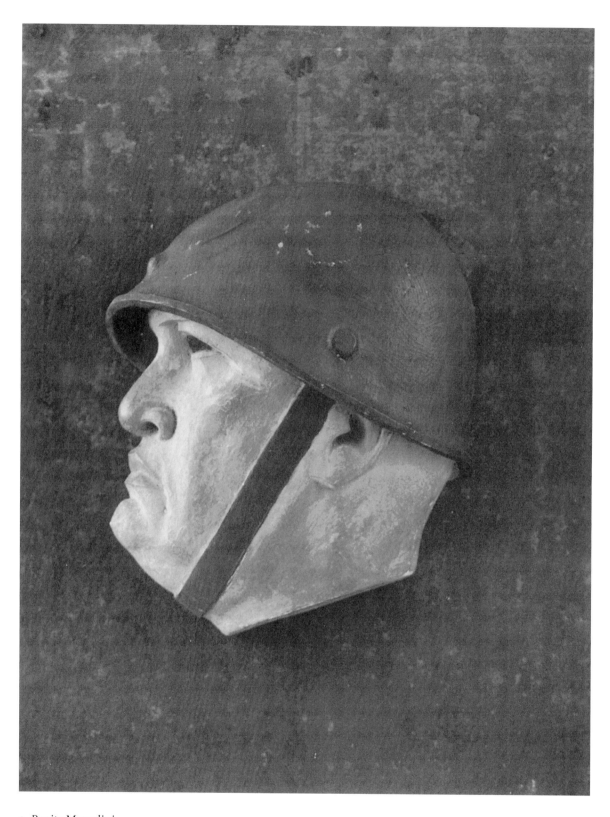

9. *Benito Mussolini*
   1930 - 34
   Polychromed plaster relief on metal
   10⅛ inches

10. *Robert E. Lee*
   1930 - 34
   Polychromed plaster
   22 ½ inches

11. *Untitled* (Figurine)
   1930 - 34
   Cast bronze and brass
   11 inches

12. *Untitled* (Figurine)
   1930 - 34
   Cast bronze
   10 ¼ inches

13. *Twentieth Century*
    1930 - 34
    Cast bronze
    19 ½ inches

14. Study for *Twentieth Century*
1930 - 34
Cast bronze
14 ½ inches

15. *The Kiss*
   1930 - 34
   Plaster (carved original)
   9 inches

16. *The Kiss*
   1930 - 34
   Cast bronze
   9 inches

17. *Torso* (female)
   1930 - 34
   Carved plaster
   22 inches

18. *Torso* (female)
   1930 - 34
   Carved mahogany
   22 inches

19. *Study*
   1930 - 34
   Terra cotta
   10 ¼ inches

20. *Slave*
1930 - 34
Terra cotta
12 ½ inches

21. *Selfish Epoch*
   1930 - 34
   Carved plaster
   17 ¾ inches

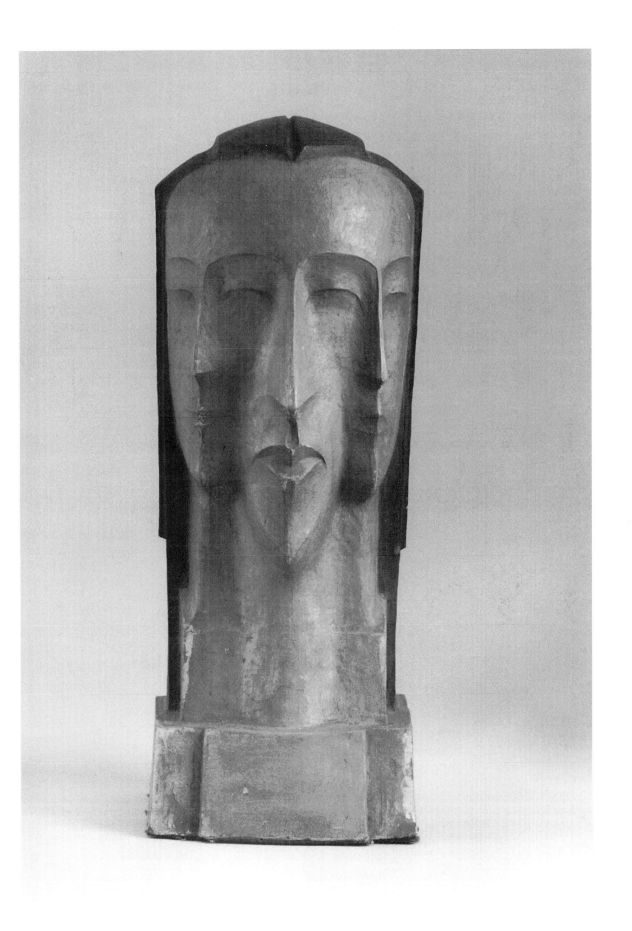

22. *Trinitas*
 1930 - 34
 Terra cotta
 13 inches

23. *Thomas Alva Edison*
   1931 - 34
   Terra cotta
   25 inches

24. *Monkey* (*the Thinker*)
  1931
  Terra cotta
  16 inches

25. *Statue to Labor*
   1933
   Terra cotta
   22¼ inches

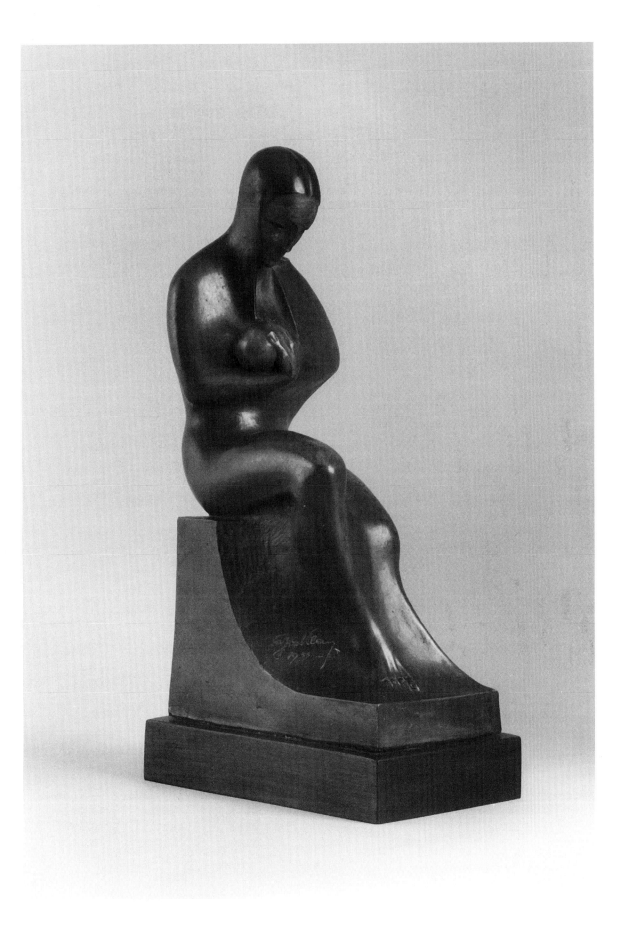

26. *Maternity*
   1933
   Terra cotta
   17 inches

27. *Wrestlers*
   1933
   Terra cotta
   10 inches

28. *Moses*
1933
Terra cotta
18 ½ inches

29. *Hand from the Cross*
    1933
    Terra cotta
    3 inches

30. *Eugene Herman Talmadge* (medallion)
   1933 - 37
   Cast bronze
   3⅜ inches

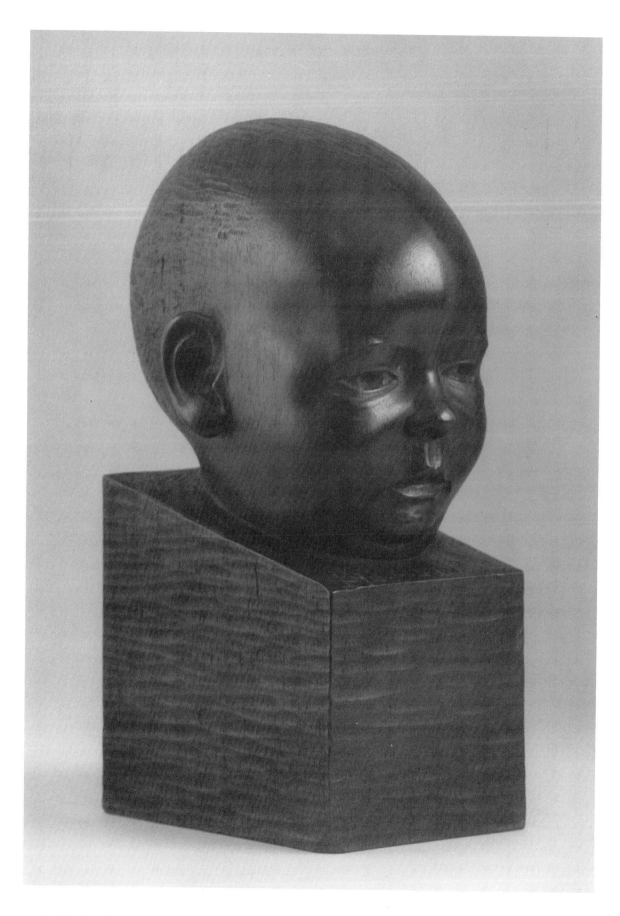

31. *Siegfried Joseph*
   1934
   Carved mahogany
   10 inches

32. *Frank L. Stanton* (tondo)
   1935
   Carved plaster
   16 inches

33. *Untitled*
   c. 1938
   Terra cotta
   9¾ inches

34. *Head of Christ*
    1939
    Cast plaster
    6 ¼ inches

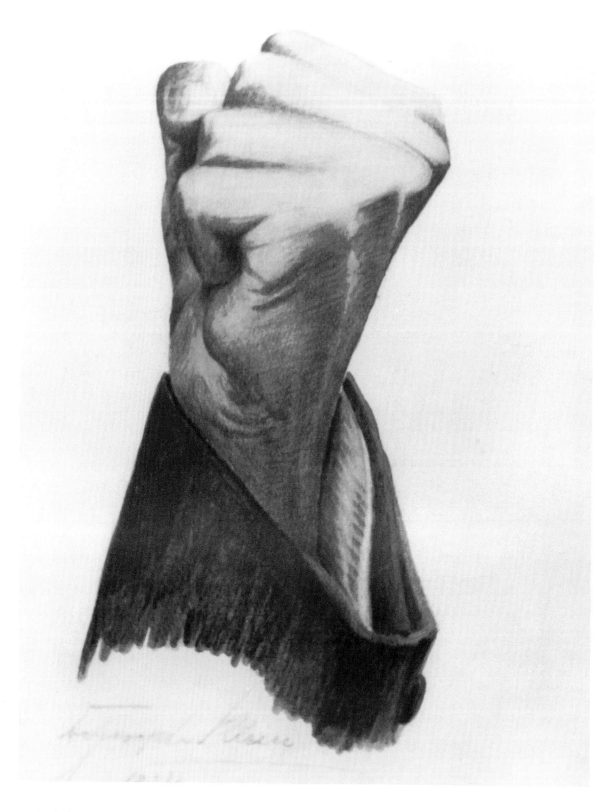

35. Study for *Thomas Watson Memorial*
    1932
    Watercolor and pencil
    13 x 10 ½ inches

36. *Untitled* (Sculptor in His Studio)
1932
Watercolor, pen, and ink
9¾ x 8¼ inches

37. *Joel Chandler Harris*
   1934
   Pencil on tracing paper
   21 x 18 inches

38. Preparatory drawing for monument to *Joel Chandler Harris* (early)
1934
Pencil on tracing paper
21 x 18 inches

39. Preparatory drawing for monument to *Joel Chandler Harris* (late)
1934
Pencil on tracing paper
21 x 18 inches

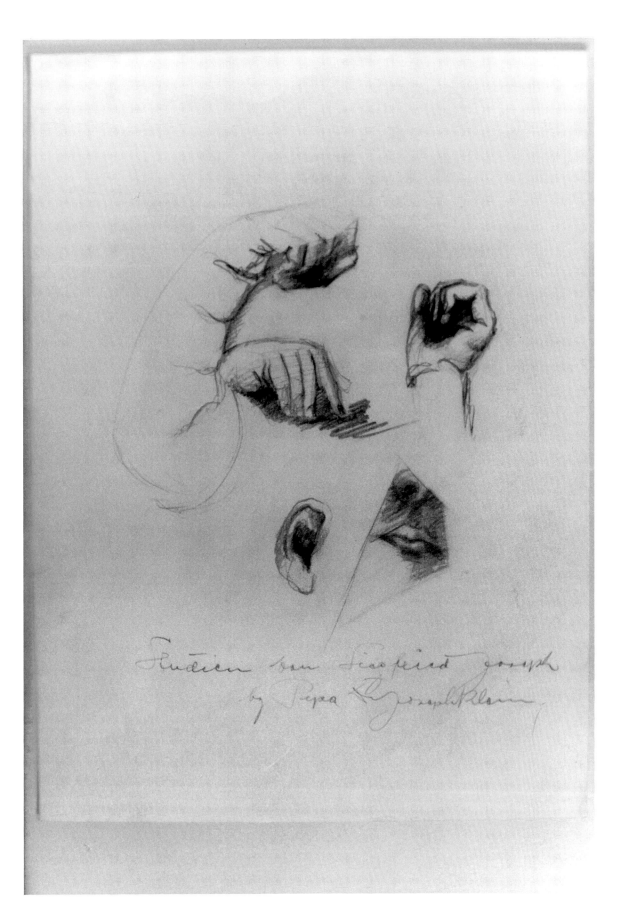

40. Study for *Siegfried Joseph*
    1934
    Pencil on tracing paper
    12 x 9 inches

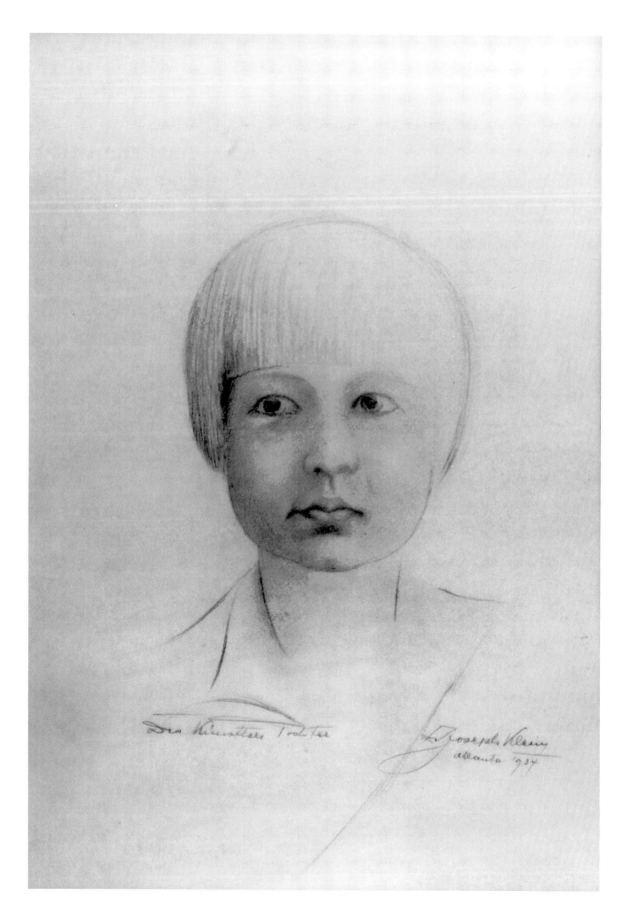

41. *The Artist's Daughter*
    1934
    Pencil on tracing paper
    21 x 18 inches

42. *Toleration*
 1934
 Pen and ink
 9 x 7½ inches

43. *Self-Portrait*
1930s
Pen and ink
9 x 6 inches

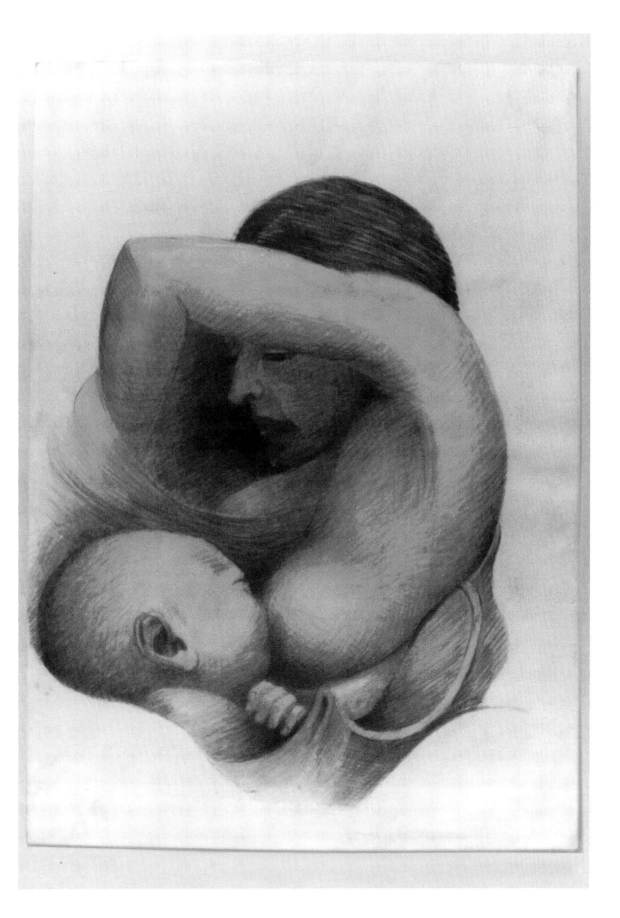

44. *Mother and Child*
    1930s
    Watercolor and pencil
    12 x 9 inches

45. *Untitled* (Sculptor in His Studio)
   1930s
   Pen and ink
   11⅛ x 8⅜ inches

46. *Untitled* (Sculptor with Child at His Studio Window)
1930s
Pen and ink
11 x 7⅜ inches

47. Site Sketch for Monumental Head of *Christ*
    1939
    Pencil on notebook paper
    7⅜ x 5⅛ inches

48. Sketch for Monumental Head of *Christ*
   1939
   Watercolor and pencil
   4½ x 4½ inches

49. *Untitled* (Portrait Fort McPherson)
1942
Pencil
14 x 10 inches

50. *Untitled* (Nude Female, Fort McPherson)

1942
Pencil
14 x 10 inches

51. *Untitled* (Standing Nude Female, Fort McPherson)
   1942
   Pencil
   14 x 10 inches

The photographs of sculptures in this catalogue were made by Nena Ducan, Houston, Texas. Photographs of drawings were made by William Squires, and prints of the drawings and several sculptures were made by Joe Cronan, Athens, Georgia.